GOVERNANCE
Committee

Berit M. Lakey,
Sandra R. Hughes,
and Outi Flynn

Book One of the BoardSource Committee Series

Formerly the National Center for Nonprofit Boards

Library of Congress Cataloging-in-Publication Data

Hughes, Sandra R.
  Governance committee / by Sandra R. Hughes, Berit M. Lakey, and Outi Flynn
    p. cm. — (Book one of The boardsource committee series)
    Includes bibliographical references.
  ISBN 1-58686-069-0 (pbk.)
  1. Boards of directors. 2. Committees. 3. Directors of corporations—Recruiting. 4. Nonprofit organizations—Management. I. Lakey, Berit M. II. Flynn, Outi. III. Title. IV. BoardSource committee series ; 1. V. Title. VI. Series.
  HD2745.H843 2004
  658.4'22—dc22
  2003022647

© 2004 BoardSource.
First printing, November 2003.
ISBN 1-58686-069-0

Published by BoardSource
1828 L Street, NW, Suite 900
Washington, DC 20036

This publication may not be reproduced without permission. Permission can be obtained by completing a request for permission form located at www.boardsource.org. Revenue from publications sales ensures the capacity of BoardSource to produce resources and provide services to strengthen the governing boards of nonprofit organizations. Copies of this book and all other BoardSource publications can be ordered by calling 800-883-6262. Discounts are available for bulk purchases.

The views in each BoardSource publication are those of its authors, and do not represent official positions of BoardSource or its sponsoring organizations.

Formerly the National Center for Nonprofit Boards

BoardSource, formerly the National Center for Nonprofit Boards, is the premier resource for practical information, tools and best practices, training, and leadership development for board members of nonprofit organizations worldwide. Through our highly acclaimed programs and services, BoardSource enables organizations to fulfill their missions by helping build strong and effective nonprofit boards.

BoardSource provides assistance and resources to nonprofit leaders through workshops, training, and our extensive Web site, www.boardsource.org. A team of BoardSource governance consultants works directly with nonprofit leaders to design specialized solutions to meet organizations' needs and assists nongovernmental organizations around the world through partnerships and capacity building. As the world's largest, most comprehensive publisher of materials on nonprofit governance, BoardSource offers a wide selection of books, videotapes, and CDs. BoardSource also hosts the National Leadership Forum, bringing together approximately 800 governance experts, board members, and chief executives of nonprofit organizations from around the world.

Created out of the nonprofit sector's critical need for governance guidance and expertise, BoardSource is a 501(c)(3) nonprofit organization that has provided practical solutions to nonprofit organizations of all sizes in diverse communities. In 2001, BoardSource changed its name from the National Center for Nonprofit Boards to better reflect its mission. Today, BoardSource has more than 15,000 members and has served more than 75,000 nonprofit leaders.

For more information, please visit our Web site at www.boardsource.org, e-mail us at mail@boardsource.org, or call us at 800-883-6262.

Have You Used These BoardSource Resources?

VIDEOS

Meeting the Challenge: An Orientation to Nonprofit Board Service
Speaking of Money: A Guide to Fund-Raising for Nonprofit Board Members
Building a Successful Team: A Guide to Nonprofit Board Development

BOOKS

The Board Chair Handbook
Managing Conflicts of Interest: Practical Guidelines for Nonprofit Boards
Checks and Balances: The Board Member's Guide to Nonprofit Financial Audits
The Board-Savvy CEO: How To Build a Strong, Positive Relationship with Your Board
Presenting: Board Orientation
Presenting: Nonprofit Financials
The Board Meeting Rescue Kit: 20 Ideas for Jumpstarting Your Board Meetings
The Board Building Cycle: Nine Steps to Finding, Recruiting, and Engaging Nonprofit Board Members
The Policy Sampler: A Resource for Nonprofit Boards
To Go Forward, Retreat! The Board Retreat Handbook
Nonprofit Board Answer Book: Practical Guide for Board Members and Chief Executives
Nonprofit Board Answer Book II: Beyond the Basics
The Legal Obligations of Nonprofit Boards
Self-Assessment for Nonprofit Governing Boards
Assessment of the Chief Executive
Fearless Fundraising
The Nonprofit Board's Guide to Bylaws
Creating and Using Investment Policies
Transforming Board Structure: New Possibilities for Committees and Task Forces

THE GOVERNANCE SERIES

1. *Ten Basic Responsibilities of Nonprofit Boards*
2. *Financial Responsibilities of Nonprofit Boards*
3. *Structures and Practices of Nonprofit Boards*
4. *Fundraising Responsibilities of Nonprofit Boards*
5. *Legal Responsibilities of Nonprofit Boards*
6. *The Nonprofit Board's Role in Setting and Advancing the Mission*
7. *The Nonprofit Board's Role in Planning and Evaluation*
8. *How To Help Your Board Govern More and Manage Less*
9. *Leadership Roles in Nonprofit Governance*

For an up-to-date list of publications and information about current prices, membership, and other services, please call BoardSource at 800-883-6262 or visit our Web site at www.boardsource.org.

Contents

Preface vii

Introduction xiii

Chapter 1:
Why Do You Need a Governance Committee? 1

Chapter 2:
Governance Committee
Membership and Operations 5

Chapter 3:
What Does a Governance Committee Do? 11

Chapter 4:
The Governance Committee's Role
in Board Recruitment and Composition 15

Chapter 5:
The Governance Committee's Role
in Orientation and Education 25

Chapter 6:
Ensuring Proper Board Performance
and Compliance 33

Conclusion 43

Appendix I:
Charge to the Governance Committee 45

Appendix II:
Sample Board Meeting Evaluation 47

Suggested Resources 48

About the Authors 51

Preface

The BoardSource Committee Series is intended to provide board members and chief executives with a practical approach to determining an appropriate committee structure and details on the responsibilities of each committee. The following preface will convey the philosophy of the series as a whole, using ideas from the first book in the series, Transforming Board Structure: Strategies for Committees and Task Forces, *and general information on how to handle committee operations.*

It is virtually impossible to define a committee structure that can or should be adopted by every nonprofit board. The material below can be used as a set of guidelines as your board searches for the best way to manage its own operations.

First and foremost, it is important to understand the difference between the full board, committees, and task forces in context of one another. The *board* has a fiduciary duty for the organization and is legally liable for its activities. It is responsible for articulating the direction for the organization and overseeing that the directives are implemented effectively and in an ethical manner. To manage these objectives, the board naturally must structure itself to accomplish its work in the most efficient manner possible.

Committees, or for the purpose of this introductory discussion, *standing committees*, are groups comprised of board members and outsiders that ensure consistency and regularity in key board practices. They are groups that are always necessary in helping the full board carry out its work. Committees (with the executive committee as a common exception) normally do not make organizational decisions; therefore, their members do not carry liability, as do members of the full board.

Task forces, similar in purpose to committees, are usually created in order to carry out a specific objective within a certain amount of time. They are typically established on an as-needed basis, allowing greater flexibility in the work of the board and its individual members. With the help of task forces, immediate needs of the board can be handled more quickly — without having to reconstruct the other committees and their ongoing work plans.

Committees and task forces generally do the majority of the board's work between meetings, allowing the full board to keep its attention on important decisions and on the big picture of the organization's success in fulfilling its mission. They give individual board members an opportunity to contribute to the work of the board in ways they would not be able to in regular meetings. These work groups enable the full board to benefit from the special skills and expertise of its members in a concrete manner.

HOW COMMITTEES ARE FORMED

To provide all the flexibility possible for your committee structure, avoid listing the job descriptions for your committees and task forces in the bylaws. A simple statement indicating that the board may form committees and other work groups as needed is sufficient. An exception to this approach, however, is the executive committee. If your board finds it necessary to form an executive committee, its authority must be detailed in your legal document. (Please refer to *Transforming Board Structure* or *Executive Committee* for more information.)

Your bylaws should also clarify who has the power to form committees. The full board should discuss and agree on the need for a specific committee or task force. Naturally, the board should also make the initial purpose of each standing committee or task force as explicit as possible to avoid any situations where the committee might establish its own charge (or description of purpose). Responsibilities of each group may shift as circumstances change, so it is important to remain flexible in each group's charge. Usually the board chair chooses each committee chair and, in collaboration, they put together the rest of the group. Some boards require the chair's appointments to be approved by the board.

It is important to clarify the distinction between *board committees* and *organizational committees* in order to avoid any misunderstanding. Board committees report to the board and help carry out its mandate.

Organizational committees, on the other hand, report to staff members and help with operational issues. They may serve as advisors to the staff and assist with issues that are staff members' responsibilities. In organizations with a small paid staff, organizational committees sometimes serve as volunteer staff to carry out the organization's work.

There is no reason for the board to duplicate staff work and form structures that collide with staff's duties. For example, if you have marketing staff, it is difficult to justify a board marketing committee. If your board includes marketing experts, there is nothing to prevent staff from asking for advice from knowledgeable board member(s) — who should be happy to oblige. If there is no staff dedicated to organizational marketing efforts, your board may consider forming a task force to look at relevant issues affecting the organization in this area. It is also possible to form an organizational committee that is more operational and composed of staff members, board specialists, and probably outsider experts.

Job Descriptions, Membership, and Size

As mentioned above, each committee or task force should have a written charter explaining its role, responsibilities, and accountability. Although the full board is responsible for agreeing on the objectives for each work group, the committee chair is responsible for leading the group in following its charter and staying focused. The committee chair communicates with the board, ensuring that appropriate reporting takes place.

It is a good idea to include varying perspectives among committee members to ensure that all aspects of an issue or task receive adequate consideration. By rotating board members in and out of different committees, the board provides possibilities for individual development. It is probably not wise, however, for an individual board member to serve on more than two committees at a time because of possible burnout. Sometimes board members who have a particular interest in learning or contributing to a specific subject or cause will request or volunteer to be on a specific committee. Additionally, not all committees are comprised solely of board members. Community leaders who can share a particular area of expertise can add to the quality of discussion. Work groups are also a great way for someone who is interested in being a board member to begin involvement with an organization. Organizational committees typically draw members from the community who can add innovation and proficiency in a specific subject. There are few committees, however, that are usually comprised of only board members (e.g., the executive committee).

When deciding on the optimal committee size, once again, no specific rule exists. It strongly depends on the purpose of the committee, scope of the task, and the size of the full board. A committee should always be small enough to keep all members thoroughly involved. Group dynamics can determine effective working relationships and consequently influence the size of the group.

Committee-Staff Relationships

Some board committees or task forces benefit from direct staff support. The chief executive can assign a staff person to relevant committees to help with background information, relate the context of the committee work to operational work, or to provide administrative support. Work groups should be careful not to inundate the staff member with unreasonable requests; after all, he or she usually has other responsibilities in addition to committee support.

Meeting Schedule, Minutes, and Reports

Determining a meeting schedule for committees or task forces should be done on an as-needed basis — there is no particular prescription for the timing and minimum or maximum meetings per year. Each group knows what is expected and must be able to determine the necessary measures to accomplish the task. With committees that have members in various areas of the country or abroad, it is possible to communicate over the telephone or electronically, as long as the desired work is getting done properly. (State laws may regulate board meetings but not committee meetings.) One frequently *ineffective* way to manage most committee meetings, however, is to schedule them in conjunction with the full board meeting in an attempt to take advantage of all members gathering in the same place at the same time. This causes repetitious conversation and agenda items and, ultimately, may be waste of time.

Each group also has the freedom to determine how to keep track of what happens in committee meetings. Work groups may or may not find it necessary to keep minutes, but most likely want to take some notes for purposes of reporting to the board or to keep track of particularly detailed information. For example, a development committee drafting action plans for the coming fiscal year will need to document decisions carefully.

It is advisable to circulate committee reports as part of the board consent agenda in the board package. This allows board members to familiarize themselves with the contents before the meeting and helps to eliminate the tradition of spending meeting time listening to committee reports. Major issues needing board debate should be placed on the main agenda.

Assessing the Need for Committees or Task Forces

In coming up with the most advantageous committee structure for your board, make sure that you continuously reassess the need for each work group. Unnecessary committees simply waste people's valuable time, misuse members' contributions and commitment, and provide no added value to the board. Some boards rely on a *zero-based committee structure*, disbanding all non-standing committees and task forces at the end of the year and reevaluating their necessity for the future — they start with a clean slate. It may still happen that a committee of the previous year gets reinstated but it may have a new composition of members or it may have a slightly changed charter. Whatever method your board uses to justify its internal structure, make sure that, ultimately, you have only committees and task forces that your organization needs and that they have all the resources necessary to function efficiently.

INTRODUCING THE SERIES

As we discussed above, there is no single right answer on how to structure a board or indicate how committees or task forces meet their expectations. Structures should never remain static and all boards should keep an open mind when experimenting with different options. Constant evaluation and flexibility are necessary during the search for optimal results. The best way to keep a committee structure simple is to limit the number of standing committees to what is absolutely essential, and to supplement these committees with less permanent structures.

With the Committee Series, BoardSource is providing additional information and guidance to help your board determine its structural options. The initial series consists of six books. The first book, *Transforming Board Structure*, sets the stage for committees in general. The next five books each cover the duties of common committees that many boards find necessary.

- *Transforming Board Structure* — introducing committee and task force structure
- *Governance Committee* (Book One) — relating to recruitment and education of board members
- *Executive Committee* (Book Two) — addressing how to use executive committees properly
- *Financial Committees* (Book Three) — defining the core duties of the finance, audit, and investment committees
- *Development Committee* (Book Four) — helping to involve your full board in fundraising
- *Advisory Councils* (Book Five) — describing the numerous roles that advisory groups or councils can play to help your nonprofit function more efficiently

Introduction

"I'm pretty sure every socially conscious person in this community has already served or been asked to serve on our board. I've run out of people to recruit!"

"Although everybody means well, our board never seems to get anything done. I think we need to change the way we work, but no one is willing to take the lead and make something happen."

"The last of our founding board members just retired, and the new folks are energetic but inexperienced with governance. We're not even sure what our bylaws say."

"Our board is filled with people who think they know all the answers because they've been on the board for years. But they're not willing to listen to any new ideas."

"We know we need some different kinds of people on the board but we're not sure where to find them."

Have any of these issues come up at your board meetings, or more likely, in the parking lot after the meeting? Does your board manage to get things done, but not as efficiently as you would like? Is your board leadership interested in preparing for the future?

If any of the above sound familiar to you as board members or chief executives, this book may help resolve these issues. Whether your board is well-established and looking to improve its effectiveness, or starting from scratch and looking for a recipe for the secret to great governance, a governance committee can help.

The following text explains the importance of including a governance committee in your board's committee structure and how to go about it. Presented as a tool for chief executives and both veteran and novice board members and board chairs, this book outlines the fundamentals of how a governance committee can help a board, and thus an organization, live up to its highest potential.

The governance committee provides the equivalent of preventative medicine to a board. This group works to ensure that a board has the right people with the right mix of skills, the most up-to-date and relevant policies, and the capacity to examine its own work and make changes when necessary. The committee can help the board when trouble arises, but its hope is that ongoing checkups and good habits will render emergencies obsolete.

Ultimately, the governance committee helps institutionalize effective governance practices for the present and future health of an organization. While it is important, be assured that the governance committee does not supercede the board in authority and in no way should it replace the board or the responsibility of all board members. It is simply a committee whose job is to help the board do its work, and to do its work better. The governance committee stays behind the scenes, making sure everything goes smoothly. The board, as always, remains the guide and compass for the organization, setting the direction for the accomplishment of essential work.

1 WHY DO YOU NEED A GOVERNANCE COMMITTEE?

Good cooks know that in order to prepare a delicious meal, they must start with the finest ingredients. In this preparation, you will need fresh food, the right combination of spices, and the right tools with which to assemble your dishes. If you are an expert chef, you need hungry diners who are willing to try something new, expecting that it will taste exquisite. Even the best chef cannot be expected to make Tournedos Rossini out of a blade cut.

You get out of it only what you put into it.

Likewise, if you want to run an outstanding nonprofit organization that does meaningful work and does it well, you need visionary leadership and a committed board (and hardworking staff, if your organization is sizeable). These elements do not just happen magically. Just as advance preparation and work are required to make a great dinner, thought and effort go into creating a great board of directors. Because boards and board members are made, not born, someone needs to act as the chef who is responsible for bringing together the right ingredients and using them in the most creative and satisfying way. In nonprofit governance, this role can be played by the governance committee of your board.

The governance committee does not run your board, but it makes it possible for the board to be run well. The governance committee can bring together the right people, help create the best policies, and stimulate provocative and forward-thinking conversation to help the board be the best it can be.

Nonprofit board members can be visionary leaders who enable their organizations to grow, achieve, and serve their communities well. Or, as chief executives often complain about, board members can be more work for staff than they seem to be worth. When the latter is the case, it is almost always because the board does not understand its roles and responsibilities. Why would board members know what they should be doing if no one tells them? Providing oversight as a board member is not a skill that comes naturally. Each board member contributes different qualities, depending on his or her experience and personality. Learning the way to proper and effective governance is similar to learning how to ride a bicycle — it is something that takes practice, patience, and most of all, time.

The following scenario illustrates what can happen, and why, when a new board member goes wrong: A nonprofit board member will contact someone she knows who shares her passion for a cause, such as animal rescue or urban parks, and ask him to join the board. Because her friend believes so strongly in these issues, and he figures he can spare one night a month for board meetings, he says yes without necessarily knowing what will be required of him. He just wants to help. That does not necessarily make him a good board member, however.

This is where the governance committee becomes so important.

The role of the governance committee is to find good, enthusiastic people with the skills needed by a particular board, to help teach these people what it means to be on a board, to continually engage them in the work of the board, to evaluate the work of the board, and to make sure the board is living up to its potential. The committee may also convey the legal side of board service and the liabilities included in it. Board candidates need to understand the seriousness with which they should undertake their service. In addition to a personal commitment of time, board members are making a legal and a financial commitment as well.

It may sound like a lot to do, but forming a great governance committee is essential in laying a solid foundation for a strong and dynamic board.

Some boards may presently have a nominating committee, or have had one in the past. This committee could be considered the ancestor of the governance committee. *Nominating committees* were primarily responsible for recruiting new members to the board. Over time, boards have discovered that such a task is more important and more time consuming than they expected, or at least it should be if done correctly. Further, effective boards realized that a committee should take the new members it has recruited and educate them about the work of the board, both in orientation sessions and throughout their tenure as board members. Discovering that it is not just new members who benefit from education about good governance — that everyone on the board finds this useful — good boards further developed a job description of this particular committee. Many boards called this new expanded nominating committee the *board development committee*. The message of its expanded role was translated, but the name of the committee still remained somewhat confusing. It became too difficult to differentiate between the board development committee and the development committee, which is responsible for involving the full board in fundraising. Thus, the original nominating committee has morphed into the *governance committee*, which provides general oversight for the health, well-being, and perpetuation of the board.

Ultimately, a good governance committee can help ward off unproductive board members, unnecessary committees, and unbearable meetings, among other unpleasant board possibilities. It exists as a committee of the board, by the board, and for the board. (Please see Appendix I for a governance committee job description.)

WHAT IF YOUR BOARD DOES NOT HAVE A GOVERNANCE COMMITTEE?

Aside from endangering the general health and future well-being of your board, not having a governance committee can damage a nonprofit in a variety of ways. Without a governance committee to do the important work of board recruitment and development, those responsibilities often remain neglected or fall to staff, creating an additional burden on a staff that is likely overworked already, trying to run essential programs effectively. Without a governance committee, the chief executive may have to handle the lion's share of board matters alone, causing a drain on his time and energy rather than having a group of the board available as a resource.

It is both unfair and inefficient to turn to the chief executive of an organization as the taskmaster for the board. The chief executive naturally is a key partner but, as a matter of hierarchy, she reports to the board. Certain board issues are better left to be handled by peers. It is more effective if a peer brings up attendance problems, behavioral divergences, or forgotten pledges. The governance committee, as a separate institution with a specific charter, is the appropriate body to address tricky issues such as these.

Of course, it is possible to have a board that happens to be brilliant and highly effective without a governance committee, but when the individuals who are leading leave the board, who knows what will happen? Making the governance committee a central and permanent part of the board structure can be key in securing the organization's viability in years to come. Most importantly, without a governance committee, the board and the organization may remain stagnant without new board members who change as the organization changes and without visionary thinking.

LIMITATIONS OF A GOVERNANCE COMMITTEE

Remember that the governance committee, as important as it may be, is not the end-all and be-all of the board. It should not expand its authority past its charter and alienate other board members. If non-committee board members have something to contribute to the governance committee on a given issue or at a particular time, they should be welcome to do so. The governance committee should not act as a replacement for the board. Committee members are **not** the only members of the board responsible for recruiting new members, being vigilant about board engagement and activity, or keeping the board working hard in governing the organization. All board members should participate in these activities, knowing that leadership and initiative in these areas will be provided by the committee. A governance committee is not a panacea, but an effective preventative tool.

2 Governance Committee Membership and Operations

Who Should Serve on a Governance Committee?

Anyone — chief executive, board chair, board member, or even a lead staff member — who sees the need for a governance committee can suggest its formation to the board. It is important to garner the support of the whole board, especially its leadership, in making a concerted effort to create an effective governance committee. Do not think you have to wait until a new year, a new fiscal year, or the next board elections to create a governance committee. A governance committee can be implemented on an as-needed basis, as long as it follows any guidelines in the board's bylaws for creating new committees. A new governance committee will have a lot of work to do, so it might as well get started as soon as possible.

If a board is structured so that its members are selected by the current board, with or without the help of the chief executive, it is quite simple to establish a governance committee. The board must be told what it is and why it is necessary, and it should be willing to give full support. After approval from the board is confirmed, the board chair can take the lead and organize the recruitment of governance committee members from among current board members and interested individuals from the outside community who have particular skills or experience with the work of governance committees.

It is important to keep in mind that the function and operations of the governance committee will depend on the size of the board, the size of this particular committee, and the role of other committees on the board. Even smaller boards benefit from the formation of a governance committee, as its role is so essential to the quality of work accomplished by the full board. After all, someone needs to remain vigilant about constant search for new blood for the board and the practices it embraces. Unlike some other board tasks, the work of the governance committee is continuous, not time limited.

Because the governance committee will, to an extent, perpetuate the board, its members should be both visionary and strategic as well as a microcosm of the board. The governance committee should include people who

- have a broad range of backgrounds
- are active in the community and in various circles

- can provide wide contacts in the community
- hold a variety of experiences
- understand human dynamics and relationship building
- have experience with organizational development
- are not afraid to speak up
- are respected by the board
- have good judgment and insight to leave a legacy to the board
- know the organization well and understand the needs of the board
- have integrity
- can leave personal agendas behind
- are willing to bring in new thoughts and perspectives — even question present practices

The governance committee can especially benefit by drawing on people with particular areas of expertise. "Naturals" for the governance committee, assuming they are willing and enthusiastic about taking on this responsibility, include management consultants and organizational development experts, human resource professionals, nonprofit executives, and community activists. Individuals with this type of experience may fall more easily into the softer side of group dynamics, organizational management, and community outreach that is necessary for the work of the governance committee.

The chair of the governance committee has a key role. In some organizations, the board automatically asks a former board chair to serve as governance committee chair. This, however, can prove to be a mistake. It is possible that a former chair might be the right person, but it is never a good idea to create an automatic succession system that does not take into account different people's varying interests and abilities. The chair of the governance committee needs to have experience with the board and the organization but not necessarily be a veteran. He or she should have plenty of energy, enthusiasm, and openness to new ideas, while maintaining an understanding of good governance practices. The chair must work closely with the chair of the full board so the governance committee is always informed by the board and aware of where it is going.

In the case that a member of the governance committee wishes to run for officer positions on the board, he should resign from the committee to prevent an unhealthy conflict of interest or even the perception of a conflict of interest. Even board members who are up for reelection should temporarily step down from the governance committee so the committee can do its work fairly without undue influence from people whose positions are at stake.

CASE STUDY: STEPPING DOWN FOR THE CAUSE

The governance committee of the board of People Who Love Animals is meeting to create the slate for officers. Jordan announces that she would like to run for the chair position. Kirk suggests that, in that case, Jordan should resign from the governance committee. Jordan disagrees, arguing that no other candidates are running against her, so why does it matter?

What is wrong with this picture?

It is a conflict of interest for Jordan to serve on the committee that is nominating her for the position of board chair. Even if there is no competition, the ethical choice would be for Jordan to step down from the committee to be considered in the officer elections. She cannot objectively decide on the best slate of candidates to serve the board and the organization if her own personal interests are at stake. Kirk is fully justified in asking Jordan to step down. If Jordan is truly committed to the well-being of the organization rather than just her own ambition or thirst for power, she will.

What now?

The chair of the governance committee may need to seek guidance from the current board chair, who might be better able to persuade Jordan to do the right thing. The governance committee may take this opportunity to hold a board discussion of ethics or governance protocol. If Jordan insists on remaining on the governance committee while she is nominated for the office of board chair, she must make sure that everyone on the board is aware of the conflict.

GOVERNANCE COMMITTEE OPERATIONS

Chief Executive Relations to the Committee

The chief executive has an important role in the activities of the governance committee. She also is greatly influenced by those who serve on the board and the quality of board members. It makes sense for the governance committee to work closely with the chief executive and take advantage of her contacts, intimate knowledge of the organization, and training abilities. However, it must be clear that the chief executive should not control the choices of the committee.

The chief executive can help the committee in the following ways:

- **Identifying the needs of the board** — The chief executive has a special perspective when looking at the composition of the board. For example, she probably wants to ensure that the board includes someone who understands the challenges of managing an organization.

- **Identifying, finding, and cultivating candidates** — The chief executive is in an excellent position to recommend candidates because of her professional links, knowledge of the field, and contacts in the community.

- **Orientation and general board education** — The chief executive is indispensable in the success of board orientation and, in general, keeping the board members on top of organizational issues. She usually knows the organization best, has access to all the necessary documents, and can ensure that everyone receives the same message.

Board development is a dynamic process and it requires an army of participants and receptive subjects. Different individuals contribute at different phases. The chief executive is a central figure during the course of action and understands that for a true collaboration to work, all partners must be well-acquainted and pursuing the same objectives.

Governance Committee and Board Chair Relations

As the person charged with general leadership of the board, the board chair stands in a special relationship to the governance committee. It is crucial that the committee and the board chair develop an open and mutually supportive relationship. A wise chair identifies ways in which the committee can support him or her in promoting board effectiveness, efficiency, and accountability. A governance committee should not shy away from proposing to the board chair improvements in operations, but must guard against taking over the chair's leadership role. Open communication between the chair of the board and the chair of the governance committee is vital for the ongoing development of the board.

The Governance Committee and the Executive Committee

Because the executive committee is given high levels of responsibility and authority, the division of labor between this work group and the governance committee may become cloudy at times. The roles of these two committees will vary depending on the leadership of the board and committee assignments, but in most cases, the executive committee has the authority to act on behalf of the full board, while the governance committee is more involved in maintaining effective overall work of the board.

On some boards, the governance committee — because of its involvement in so many aspects of the board's work — may take on roles that do not belong to it. It may turn into a semiexecutive committee or, at least, be perceived to have assumed that powerful role. It is important that the committee functions in total openness, does not pretend to make board decisions or have full board authority, and invites feedback from all board members who are concerned about the way the board is functioning.

Other Committees of the Board

The full board *must* be clear on the necessity of specific committees, as has already been discussed in the preface of this book. The governance committee can be very helpful in suggesting other committee structures, assignments, and communication methods between and among committees and the full board. When assessing the overall committee issues, separate task forces may be formed to handle the actual work that the governance committee suggests as necessary. The governance committee is not the "boss" of other committees of the board; it should simply be available to help with any necessary restructuring, operational changes, and assignment of members.

When Is the Governance Committee Called To Work?

The short answer is: all the time, year round. There is always something the governance committee can be doing to prepare the board for its work and to ensure board members are educated about their roles and responsibilities. In the long run, the governance committee may be the *most important* committee of the board because of its responsibility for the long-term success of the board and, in turn, of the organization.

While varying committee structures suggest different ideas for what committees a board should include and for how long, there should always be a governance committee. Committee members may rotate and the goals of the committee may change from year to year, but the committee should remain standing to ensure the good work of the board. As the conscience of the board, the governance committee should be a keen observer of the way the full board works, and charged with finding ways to improve operations; thus, increasing the job satisfaction of all board members.

The frequency of governance committee meetings depends on the individual board and the level of work the governance committee is doing at any time. Remember not to saddle board and committee members with too many meetings per month. That said, the committee may meet as little as quarterly or as often as monthly. It may meet on a less or more regular schedule depending on the time of year and the tasks at hand. Several months before board seats are expected to be vacated, the governance committee should be working its hardest to ensure a great pool of candidates will be available for recruitment.

3 WHAT DOES A GOVERNANCE COMMITTEE DO?

Ultimately, the governance committee adds value to the board by institutionalizing best practices in board governance for the board to follow. It is one of several components of good governance. The governance committee oversees each step in the board building cycle, which includes the following nine steps to having a great board:

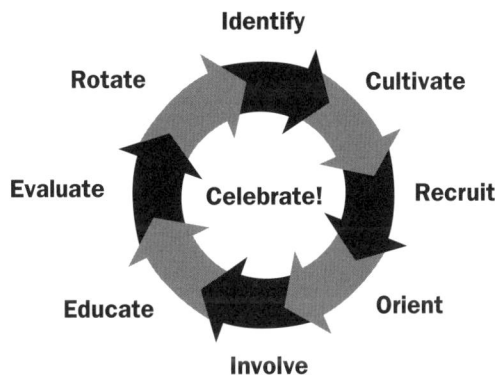

It is responsible for seeing that all of these pieces of board building are incorporated into the full board's practices. (See *The Board Building Cycle* in Suggested Resources.)

WHAT BOARD ISSUES ARE IMPORTANT TO THE GOVERNANCE COMMITTEE?

While the work of the governance committee should take place throughout the year, not just when new board members are needed, the majority of the work may come when the committee is first established. However, to avoid overwhelming a brand new committee with a daunting task, the work may be spread out over time and each task taken as it comes in the course of regular business. Eventually, when the committee has worked through the first round of its basic responsibilities, it should consider its scope of work as a routine checkup on the health of the board.

Meanwhile, here are some of the questions the governance committee should ask itself in order to decide what work needs to be done. As stated earlier, the governance committee may not be involved in implementing these tasks but it ensures that the board pays proper attention to the following issues:

- Does the composition of the board reflect the needs of the board today and in the future?

- Do board members know what is expected of them?

- Do board members have a thorough and up-to-date board handbook?

- Do board members feel comfortable talking to outsiders (especially potential new board members) about the organization? Have they had an opportunity to role-play or practice talking about the organization in case they are called on to do so?

- Do board members know when all board and organizational meetings and events are taking place?

- Does the board engage in regular assessments of its meetings? Is attendance good and consistent at meetings? Do all board members participate? Do they seem interested? Are discussions lively? Has the board offered board members a chance to comment on the effectiveness of the meetings?

- Does the board have term limits? If not, why not? If so, are they effective at bringing new perspectives to the table and removing burned-out board members?

- Has the board asked individual board members to assess their own performance and given them an opportunity to provide feedback on the overall workings of the board? Do all board members feel listened to and do they have sufficient opportunities to contribute without being overwhelmed by demands from the board?

- Has the board engaged in a self-assessment in the past five years? If not, why not? If yes, what were the results and have problem areas been followed up on? What did the board learn? Is it time for another self-assessment? If it is not, what can the board do in the meantime to check up on its own performance? Does the board need to organize a retreat in order to discuss the results of a board self-assessment or to explore other ways of improving board effectiveness?

- Has the board done succession planning to prepare for unexpected leadership transitions on the board? Has the board discussed transition planning with senior staff and with board members?

- Have the organization's bylaws been updated recently? Do they cover such emerging issues as technology and how it may relate to voting and meeting procedures? Do they include irrelevant information that could be discarded? Are board and staff aware of what is in the bylaws and do they follow them?

The governance committee does not work in a vacuum; it is involved with a board operating in a constantly changing environment. Group dynamics, overall organizational evolution, and forthcoming challenges dictate the manner and focus of the committee's operations. The key to successful accomplishment of the governance committee's duties is the realization that work is not done for today but that, with an eye on the next years to come, the committee is building a board that is able to take its responsibility in securing the future of the organization.

CHALLENGES FACING THE GOVERNANCE COMMITTEE

A committee that is as involved as the governance committee cannot expect every day to run smoothly. Because it acts as the motivator of the full board to participate in board business, a misunderstanding of this role by other members of the board can create many challenges. Governance committee members are not and should not be the only board members concerned with, paying attention to, or participating in recruitment. Just as most development committees struggle with other board members washing their hands of their own fundraising responsibilities because "the development committee is supposed to take care of it," the governance committee is often expected to fulfill actions and responsibilities that fall to the entire board. The governance committee, however, exists to *establish* and *guide* the process of recruitment and orientation, but the actual finding and training of new board members remains the responsibility of each board member.

Similarly, the governance committee should work closely with the chief executive in finding new board members (as discussed on page 8), but this task should never be left to the chief executive to accomplish on her own. The committee is accountable for its own work but it should understand the needs of the chief executive and incorporate them in the objectives of the committee. Most chief executives have a strong motivation to see a responsive board in place, with which they can work without conflict. They have an incentive to participate in the board-building process but they should not be left with the full task. This would lead the chief executive to select her own supervisors, creating an explicit conflict of interest. Every chief executive can add a different perspective to defining board composition and committee members should be grateful for this level of assistance.

Few boards are composed of members who are perpetually active, on the right track, and eager to be constantly involved. Engagement tends to be a perennial board problem. It becomes a challenge for the governance committee, which must be inventive and persuasive on a regular basis — taking the role of solving this constant problem. Some specific ways to get board members reconnected, such as conducting a self-assessment, are discussed further in Chapter 6.

4. THE GOVERNANCE COMMITTEE'S ROLE IN BOARD RECRUITMENT AND COMPOSITION

Few boards find it possible to rejuvenate themselves without effort. A governance committee is the perfect tool for the full board, taking on the responsibility of ensuring that the board's composition is in sync with the expectations placed on it at any given moment. A concerted effort to bring in the right board members is most effectively accomplished through coordination by individuals who are best equipped for the task.

TRY THIS!

Who can or should do what?

The committee is involved with numerous activities that all relate to recruitment, orientation, or other major board development or process issues. Individual committee members can enhance their personal involvement by volunteering to

- collect and manage files for board member applications and resumes
- keep a file of newspaper clippings or other information about potential board members for future reference
- host an open house for interested board members on site
- invite candidates to other organizational events — and pay their way if fees are involved
- interview board member candidates with a peer or the chief executive

---

BOARD RECRUITMENT

While recruitment is by no means the only responsibility of the governance committee, it may be the most important because of the far-reaching effects recruiting the right (or wrong) board members can have on the organization. Recruitment starts with identifying possible candidates and cultivating them until they become promising prospects.

When recruiting, the entire board must be involved, but the governance committee should spearhead the effort by carefully planning ahead. The first step of recruitment is developing a board recruitment matrix.

This is simply a chart that includes information about the skills, characteristics, and attributes needed on the board according to the strategic direction in which your organization is heading. Be sure to include in the matrix every possible kind of person and ability from which your board could benefit. For example, if your organization serves homeless families, should your board have

- at least one formerly homeless person on the board?
- young people?
- police officers?
- medical professionals?
- mental health experts?
- substance abuse or addictions specialists?
- representatives from collaborating nonprofits and congregations?
- a mix of ages and socioeconomic backgrounds?
- different perspectives from the community?
- different ethnic groups?
- business leaders?
- government leaders?

Of course it is not necessary to have a member from each of these groups, but it is necessary to brainstorm extensively about the different kinds of people whose resources, ideas, and attitudes would bring something valuable to your board. Perhaps these people are radically different from the individuals who have willingly served on the board in the past. You may not have to overhaul your board, but you should consider widening the scope of whom you recruit.

CASE STUDY: WHOM TO RECRUIT

Governance committee members are in the middle of a heated debate. Should we send solicitations for board members to targeted corporations and organizations? The group is divided into two camps. One argues that a campaign like that merely produces warm bodies. The other side insists that such a method allows the governance committee to amass a pool of candidates from which to cull great board members.

What is wrong with this picture?

Nothing may be wrong at all, assuming governance committee members are conducting the debate in a fair and constructive way. Conflict, handled well, can be healthy and productive for any board or committee. And it is a good problem to have when you have more than one plausible idea about how to recruit new board members.

What now?

Why not try more than one approach in your recruitment? Traditionalists can use the tried and true technique of cultivating individual relationships and inviting those with potential to serve on the board. Meanwhile, a few of the innovative thinkers can come up with two or three institutions on which to try their new idea. Allow a reasonable amount of time for connections to be made — giving all potential board members the same information and opportunities to learn about the organization and the board — and see if the new plan bears fruit.

Where To Look for New Board Members

Now, where do you find these people who you have just determined are the future of your board? Current board members, committee members, and staff can help by throwing in recommendations for specific people, as well as where to look for other possibilities. The governance committee guides this recruitment process and gives board members tools and resources to conduct it.

It will also be helpful to explore the following places for possible recruits:

- institutions that could offer useful perspectives on the societal issues tackled by your organization, such as local government, law enforcement, or health clinics

- churches, synagogues, mosques, or other religious institutions

- trade or professional associations

- ethnic and cultural organizations
- community and civic organizations
- local colleges and universities
- volunteer centers

Many people who do not volunteer regularly for nonprofit organizations say they would like to help, and would be willing to help if someone asked them. When board members start contacting people in order to get to know and engage them with service on their organization's board, they need to go into it with the right attitude. The governance committee should demonstrate to the board various ways to make the pitch, providing a training session for everyone — especially those who will do the inviting. Too often board candidates are approached as if being asked for a favor, presenting board service as a chore rather than an opportunity to contribute to the community. Instead, it is important to stress the essential nature of the board's work in the community. Demonstrate to these candidates the opportunity to serve within the community and work with others who share common values. Explain why the organization, the community, and the candidate would all benefit from the person's service on your board. The governance committee should make sure those doing the recruiting are well-versed in the organization's mission and current programs so they can explain the importance of what the board and organization do with a sense of pride.

Ideally, prospecting for future board members should not wait until a new election is looming on the horizon. The approach should be to explore a potential candidate's interest and ability to serve when and if there is an opening during the next year or two. Remember that the committee identifies viable candidates, but it is the board that elects.

BOARD COMPOSITION

Creating a Balanced Board

What Are the Benefits of a Balanced Board?

Diversity has become a buzzword, which some people embrace and others resist. Instead of diversity, we prefer the term *balance* or *inclusiveness*, which suggests that a board should find ways to get input from everyone who has a stake in the organization and could improve its effectiveness. While boards do not necessarily need a board member who represents each of their stakeholder groups, it may be useful to create more

> ### CASE STUDY: HOW DO I CONTACT PROSPECTS?
>
> *Different members of the governance committee seem to have widely differing methods of approaching prospective board members. Carmen gathers handfuls of brochures and other materials to present before she talks to someone. Antoine is willing to make phone calls but doesn't want to meet face-to-face with prospects. Diya is so exceptionally enthusiastic about working with prospects that she sends them the message that every candidate is almost automatically elected.*
>
> **What's wrong with this picture?**
>
> It looks like every potential board member is getting a completely different impression of the board, its culture, and perhaps even of the organization. This can be dangerous because it may lead to a board filled with people who are not adequately prepared to serve or who come to the table with unrealistic expectations.
>
> **What now?**
>
> Harness all that energy and get everyone on the same page. Provide the full board with a training session, perhaps led by an outside facilitator, on how to talk about both the organization and board service. Make sure everyone understands the recruitment process and agrees to follow it. Pair up individuals into teams according to their strengths. Two heads can be better than one and a partnership may be able to recruit new board members more effectively by sharing the work and telling the story together.

balanced leadership in the organization by including a wide variety of people on the full board and/or on committees and advisory councils.

A board composed entirely of people with similar backgrounds, interests, skills, and demographics may be nearsighted. It may enjoy always finding agreement about the issues at hand and may never experience conflict. This outcome, however, will cause the board to miss the benefit of different perspectives that push board members to rethink their positions or explore new ideas. Inclusiveness brings a variety of attitudes, opinions, approaches, and solutions. It moves away from the "friends of the board" approach, which draws on the same or similar pool of support, and helps reach further into the community, broadening the entire base of support. Having an inclusive board will make decision making more challenging, but also more thorough.

The reality of an inclusive board mirrors the values and culture of the organization. It sends a message to other organizations and sets an example within the organization. It shows that inclusiveness is important and not just a policy or a statement, but an important way to run an organization.

Many constituents expect boards to reflect the demographic composition of those the organization serves, but few boards usually fully accomplish this. An inclusive board creates a sense of community leadership and gives constituents a link with the board and the feeling that the board really has their best interests at heart. It is important that the board understands the issues and concerns of the constituents but composing the board only of people representing those served by the organization may not always provide all the skills and expertise needed.

While the governance committee is working on forming a diverse board, it should not make each person feel like a poster child for the group whose opinions it is supposedly representing. Even the best intentions toward inclusiveness can sometimes result in tokenism if proper care is not taken. No person is able to or should be required to represent an entire segment of the population. The following box provides guidelines on how to avoid tokenism when recruiting new board members.

HOW TO AVOID TOKENISM

- Announce your board's commitment to diversity and put it in writing.

- Recruit more than one person from a particular demographic at the same time.

- Involve every new member immediately and personally.

- Focus on the board as a diverse mixture, not on the individual representation of each member.

- Once new members are elected, treat each board member the same and expect the same effort from each board member.

- Give each board member, whether a novice or a veteran, clear responsibilities.

- Assign tasks independent of cultural or ethnic background while still respecting individual differences and preferences.

What Is the Next Step to Creating a Balanced Board?

As the governance committee leads the way in seeking a balanced board, the next step is to take an inventory of the individuals who are currently serving on the board. This may seem obvious, but it is worthwhile to ask these board members what their skills and interests are. Board and committee members may have assumed for years that the accountant on the board loves serving as treasurer, but his event-planning skills may have been overlooked in the process. What people do in their professional lives may or may not accurately reflect their passions in the boardroom. It cannot hurt to ask them what they like to do, or, with a little training, what they would like to learn to do. Make sure the full board agrees on what is needed so that each new candidate has a good idea of what is expected of him from the outset, and can decide easily whether he fits the bill. In seeking to form a balanced board, it is also important to look to the future and consider gaps created by those who will have completed their term of service.

TRY THIS!

At the end of a board meeting, ask every board member to write down *all* the reasons why he or she decided to accept this board appointment or why he or she has determined to stay on. Compile the results for the next meeting and discuss the comments together. You will have a quick analysis on the overall satisfaction level and what actually drives your board members to stay committed.

Attracting New Board Members from the Next Generation

Studies have been done and books have been written about the characteristics of the post-Baby Boom generations. This next generation of leaders has some different needs, preferences, and desires than their parents and grandparents. Sooner or later these individuals will be running your organization and your board. It is time to get to know them and benefit from their energy and ideas now. Chances are they will bring great passion and energy to the work of the board.

So how do you find these young people and how do you keep them excited about your work? Look in unusual places. Young professionals or older students (or youth, if your organization serves them) can make terrific contributions to the board if they are asked. Young people are often attracted to short-term, project-specific work. Inviting them to help with a special event or particular campaign can be a great way to

Case Study: What If You Forget To Cultivate?

The annual meeting of the Mountain Villages Preservation Society is coming up in January. It is now the end of November. Three seats on the nine-person board will be vacated as of the January meeting, and members of the society expect to receive a slate of candidates for the board seats on whom they will vote in January.

Suddenly realizing how time has slipped away, the chair of the governance committee, Jacqueline Eyre, hurriedly sends a meeting notice to committee members and asks everyone to bring along a list of candidates.

What's wrong with this picture?

Jacqueline and her committee have not kept active all through the year looking for new board member candidates but seem to wake up just before the annual meeting and looming board elections. It is difficult to create a slate of candidates when forced to make choices without careful search and preparation. Cultivation is an ongoing, year-round activity. A board profile grid or matrix could help the committee focus on needed skills and characteristics that will be lost when the terms end for the three board members. The committee should keep a pool of candidates at all times.

The committee should actively communicate with the various constituents of the Society and get their feedback and suggestions for suitable candidates. The remaining board members should also be invited to provide ideas and leads. The aim should be to locate numerous prospects — maybe some of them would not be ready or willing to step in until the following year's elections.

Other preparations with which the committee should be involved right now is to verify all the orientation materials and to work with the chief executive for the annual meeting planning.

What now?

Rather than crying over spilled milk, Jacqueline can do one of two things. One — convince the governance committee to put in some serious effort over the next month and a half developing a board matrix and asking members to suggest outstanding candidates. Do everything right, but do it fast.

Or, take the time needed to do the work in a more thoughtful and deliberate way, and put off the election until a later time. It might be better to leave those seats empty for a few months while you implement a solid process for the future, than to fill them with people thrown together at the last minute. This will depend, of course, on the requirements stated in the bylaws and the board's decision to postpone the election.

introduce them to the organization and get them invested. Then invite them to serve on a committee for a finite amount of time. If these young recruits remain committed to the work of the organization and demonstrate the skills and qualifications your committee and board are looking for, ask them to consider a term on the board.

Young people also have a lower tolerance for long, dull meetings, and are usually confident that "the way it's always been done" is not necessarily the best way. Their fresh personal and professional experiences color their perspective on how to get things done in the most effective way. Keeping board meetings relevant, efficient, and productive will likely keep young board members involved.

THE GOVERNANCE COMMITTEE AND MEMBERSHIP ORGANIZATIONS

In membership organizations, particularly associations, the governance committee has a demanding role. In a case where board members are elected by the members of the association, the governance committee must work to inform members on the needs of the organization for a multifaceted and unbiased board, and on what special qualities and characteristics candidates should have if they are nominated by members. It must then prepare the slate of candidates. The governance committee may serve as a liaison between the members and the candidates, or in general matters, between the members and the board.

Once the governance committee has compiled a slate of candidates, it should publicize this list of people and provide plenty of information about them and their qualifications to the entire membership. The committee should disseminate this information well in advance of the election whether this takes place at the annual meeting or through different channels such as e-mail and regular mail. The bylaws or policies of the organization may describe specific requirements.

A good governance committee will present the candidates in a fair and balanced way, as well as presenting the needs of the board and the direction of the organization, so members can vote for those who are best qualified to move the board forward instead of making board elections a popularity contest. The members have a challenge to put aside their personal preferences and look at the collectivity of the candidates and the instructions that the governance committee has distributed. This board will have to lead the organization objectively without a bias in one direction or another. To assist association members in electing a balanced board, it will be helpful also to send out information about the continuing members of the board.

In federated organizations where chapter representatives are nominating national board members, the governance committee must stress that the members are voting for people who will best govern the national organization and focus on its interests rather than on the interests of local affiliates. The board will concentrate on major issues that address national strategy for the organization. It cannot get bogged down by details affecting individual affiliates but it must be receptive to their perspectives. Only a well-tuned board is able to advance the business that benefits every chapter in the federation.

5. The Governance Committee's Role in Orientation and Education

Bringing promising and eager board members into your boardroom is an excellent start — but leaving them on their own to figure out what to do next is poor risk management and waste of good potential. The governance committee must take charge and ensure that orientation is part of the board's practices, and that even the ideas of seasoned board members are continuously refreshed.

Creating an Overall Effective Board

New Board Member Orientation

Orientation should be held before each board member attends his or her first board meeting to help this new individual start contributing as soon as possible. The orientation session, which should be planned by the governance committee, can be crafted according to individual needs and organizational culture, but should include several key board members and at least the chief executive. New board member orientation should be 50 percent about the organization and its programs and services, and 50 percent about each board member's understanding of his or her role as a member of the board.

The following list describes information that should be conveyed to new board members at their orientation. This material can be presented in person or in writing, and may require more than one session in order to avoid information overload:

- **Program:** It is important to get new board members emotionally and intellectually connected to the organization. Give them a feel for what the organization does, whom it serves, and what difference it makes. This can be done in many ways, including giving them a tour of facilities, allowing them to observe program activities, introducing them to a client or member, and giving them written materials about past and present programs.

- **Finances:** New board members need to know where money comes from, how it is spent, the state of the organization's financial health, and their role in fundraising. It may help to organize a presentation by the chief financial officer or treasurer, and to present new members with recent financial materials (e.g., budget forecast, recent audit, fundraising strategy). New members also need to be taught how to read the financial statement.

- **History:** For the present to make sense, new board members should know about the organization's past. Give them photographs, written materials, and "old timers'" stories in order to help them understand the history. Do not overlook the crises or hard times in the past.
- **Strategic Direction:** In providing a framework for effective participation, clarify the mission, vision, organizational values, and goals to inspire organizational actions. It will be helpful to give new members a copy of the mission statement and/or strategic plan.
- **Organizational Structure:** New members should become familiar with who does what in the organization. They should be introduced to senior staff members and receive a copy of the organizational chart.
- **Board Roles:** The full board should take part in a group discussion to ensure that new members understand the roles of the board.
- **Board Member Responsibilities:** In order to assist new members in understanding their individual responsibilities as board members, they should be presented with a job description as well as a letter of agreement, and a conflicts of interest and ethics statement for them to sign.
- **Board Operations:** For new members to understand board operations, they should be presented with a copy of the bylaws, board manual, committee charges and member lists, and a meeting schedule. They should also be introduced to their individual board mentor.
- **Board Members:** The best way to get new members integrated is to present them with a list of board members and their biographical data, and facilitate a social interaction time.

One great way to get board members involved right away and help them feel comfortable is by providing board mentors — pairing an experienced board member with a novice one. Governance committee members should ensure that each mentor contacts the new board member after meetings to answer questions. Mentors should generally serve as a resource to new board members, introducing them in the community, if necessary, and helping them get acclimated to the culture of the board. It also may be effective to treat the new group of board members as an incoming "class of 200X." Create a social event or mixer as part of the orientation.

CASE STUDY: SEPARATION OF CURRENT AND NEW BOARD MEMBERS

Board member orientation has been scheduled for next Friday afternoon from noon to four. Lunch is being served. Three new members of the board of Elmo's Kitchen are being trained. The whole board has been invited to attend. Veteran board members complain that they have to go even though they already know what the organization is doing.

What's wrong with this picture?

Rather than requiring experienced board members to attend an orientation session as spectators and sit through a presentation they have probably memorized, include them in the planning and implementation of the orientation. Veteran board members can be invaluable resources in orienting new board members. They can serve as mentors to individual members. They can present a panel discussion on "If I Had Known Then What I Know Now." They can help the governance committee come up with a variety of ways to engage new board members and inform them of the most important elements of board service.

What now?

There is still time to include experienced voices in the orientation. Ask veteran board members to think of wisdom to share and fit two or three short activities into your agenda, spread throughout the session, where people can share what they have learned. These could even happen during lunch, and can serve as icebreakers or get-to-know-you exercises that will help the new board become comfortable as a unit.

Keeping the Board Fresh

Even the most well-meaning and innovative individuals can eventually run out of good ideas. Sustaining an excited and vigorous board is work that may be shared by the board chair and governance committee. The governance committee is responsible for making sure the board stays balanced with the right people in the right positions. There are a variety of ways to keep a board dynamic and interesting.

Guide the board to reassign committee membership. Do you need new people on your committees? Consider people from outside the board to infuse new ideas. Have the same people served on or chaired the same committees for years? Politely and graciously ask them if they would consider leading in a new capacity and reassign them. Make sure the chairs of each committee receive training and continuing education about their committee focus areas. Ensure that they are involved in recruiting great new members as well.

Suggest the board create ad hoc committees or task forces. When a special issue comes up that will not likely remain part of the board's work indefinitely, create an ad hoc committee or task force to address it. These short-term assignments are ideal for new people from outside the organization whom you are trying to get more involved. By integrating new people into some of the board's work without requiring full board membership, you can expose them to the work of the board while giving them a chance to concentrate on a time-limited project that can provide more immediate satisfaction and is not as significant a commitment.

Draft processes for rotating board leadership. Nowhere is it written in stone that the board officers must be the oldest members of the board. Nor is it necessary that the treasurer be an accountant or that the vice-chair will eventually become the next chair. Shake up the board leadership if necessary. Find rising stars to take key positions. Divide up responsibility so newer or younger board members are not intimidated by the prospect of serving as a board officer. Depending on the election process outlined in the organization's bylaws, you may be able to ask current officers to serve in other capacities so you don't lose their wisdom and experience but your board still benefits from new perspectives.

Design ways to send board members outside to represent your organization. Board members may be energized and honored when you ask them to serve as official ambassadors for your organization in the community. This could mean becoming a spokesperson for the organization at community events or with the media. Make sure anyone whom you ask to serve in these capacities has training and is thoroughly knowledgeable about the work of the organization.

Try This!

Ask all board members — new and more seasoned ones — to write down three issues with which they would like to work. Don't limit their options to already existing activities. These comments may provide your governance committee with totally new ideas for activities and clarify the true interests of your board members. It can make it easier to recommend committee and task force assignments without making "obvious" assumptions.

Continuous Education of the Board

Individual Board Member Responsibilities

A common complaint of board members, both novice and veteran, is that they do not entirely understand what their responsibilities are. The governance committee should provide board members with specific and clear descriptions of all board members' roles and responsibilities, and give board members a chance to ask questions. They should accomplish this by keeping the laws, policies, and procedures at hand, acting as the reminder for the full board.

Authority in a nonprofit organization generally resides in the board as a corporate body. In other words, no board member can individually be responsible for the work or actions of the whole board. However, when a person agrees to serve on a board, she is assuming some responsibilities for the organization. The bylaws should specify duties that fall under specific board offices. Board members are expected to comply with certain legal standards. These are commonly known as the duties of care, loyalty, and obedience.

Duty of Care: Also called the "business judgment rule," the duty of care is the "care that an ordinarily prudent person would exercise in a like position and under similar circumstances." What this really means is participate and **pay attention**. Stay informed and ask questions. Read the minutes you are signing off on and familiarize yourself with board materials and background information for board discussions. Participate in deliberations and understand what is being said and agreed upon. If board members do not understand, they should keep asking questions until they do.

Duty of Loyalty: When an individual joins a board, he is basically pledging his allegiance to the organization. Being loyal means he is faithful to the organization, promoting its welfare and best interests. Members should not be personally profiting financially or enabling others who are close to them to benefit from board decisions. All boards should have a conflict-of-interest statement that board and staff sign annually to disclose personal and business affiliations that might cause potential conflicts and interfere with an individual's fidelity to the organization. Board members should also disclose relevant potential conflicts in board discussions and recuse themselves from votes when necessary.

Duty of Obedience: Complying with the duty of obedience means that each member agrees to support the organization in its mission and work. While boards do make policy decisions that set new strategic directions for an organization, the board members' responsibility is to keep the work of the board and the organization consistent with the mission and purpose of the organization as best they can. This duty is designed to ensure that an organization's supporters know their contributions will be used in accordance with the organization's stated mission. Duty of obedience also expects board members to follow the bylaws and state and federal laws governing the organization.

Ensuring Accuracy and Implementation of Board Member Job Descriptions

Nobody would hire someone to work for his or her company without telling him what his responsibilities are. Why would you ask someone to perform a significant and long-term volunteer leadership position without explaining what she needs to do? Before recruitment begins, the governance committee should ensure that accurate board member job descriptions are in place. When the board is facing election or appointment of new board officers, the committee should also create board officer job descriptions.

A board member job description should include

- the organization's mission and the explicit expectation that board members should support it
- approximate number of board meetings, committee meetings, or other events that board members are required to attend
- the expectation that board members will review materials circulated in preparation for meetings
- how board members are expected to communicate with the board (e.g., via e-mail if that is the board culture)
- how board members are expected to participate in meetings and decisions
- how much money board members are expected to contribute or help raise
- how board members are expected to comply with board policies

Officer job descriptions can include any responsibilities specific to the office, such as taking minutes, preparing financial statements, or chairing meetings. Often, staff members are responsible for some of these tasks, but in smaller organizations they may fall to board officers.

Turning Great Board Members into Effective Leaders

Just as skillful board members can be taught (and are rarely born that way), board leaders can be trained. Certainly there are some people who everyone agrees are natural leaders, and it is wonderful to have articulate, organized, efficient, fair, and charismatic people present themselves, offering to serve as board officers. If this does not happen on its own, however, the governance committee can play an important role in growing board leadership.

Employees are often given opportunities for professional development, and so should board members. Governance committee members can help by finding out what organizations in the area offer workshops in governance issues. State associations for nonprofit organizations, management and technical assistance providers, or volunteer centers are great places to start. National organizations (like BoardSource) also hold regional workshops that provide board education. If there are particular board members with great passion and potential, governance committee members should talk to them about how to best develop their governance expertise. Are they worried about chairing meetings or understanding finances? Help each board member develop the skills and competencies necessary to become a well-rounded board leader. Pair emerging leaders with mentors on the board (or former board members) who can offer them guidance. Let emerging leaders practice for board leadership by asking them to chair committees or be in charge of special board activities. Give people who want to learn every opportunity to do so.

From a pool of potential leaders it is easy to select the next officers for the board. The traditional voting mechanism relies on the governance committee to prepare a slate of candidates. If the committee reflects the composition of the board and is fair and open-minded, it has a chance to create a sensible slate. When this is the case, board members can consider its recommendations well-founded and sound. Through open discussion, the board makes the final choice from the slate. If the governance committee has not earned the trust of the rest of the board members, or the role of the committee is unclear, officer election can turn into unnecessary confrontation and a game of choosing winners and losers. The same holds for the development of new board member slates.

Another method for electing officers is for the governance committee to facilitate the process. The committee will collect nominations from board members, communicate back and forth with candidates, and recommend one candidate who emerges as the best choice for each position. Finally, the full board confirms the committee's selection.

In some membership organizations, the corporate members, besides electing the board, may elect the officers. As it is much easier for board members to assess the qualifications of candidates and the needs of the board than for the entire membership to bear this responsibility, it makes sense to strengthen the role of the governance committee in the eyes of the members. Explain the role of the committee and show that the members can trust its recommendations.

6 ENSURING PROPER BOARD PERFORMANCE AND COMPLIANCE

Because the full board is constantly involved in maintaining effective oversight and proper planning for the needs of its organization, it is easy to forget the importance of managing its own performance. The governance committee is charged with making certain that the full board runs efficiently and ethically. It might recommend that a line item be included in the organization's budget for board development that can be used to bring in consultants, send board members to trainings, provide coaching for the board chair, hold a retreat, and implement other board development efforts that would strengthen the performance of the board. When focusing on specifics, it is important to study the effectiveness of board meetings — where the board ultimately does its business — and the best ways of evaluating board operations and ensuring compliance to the mission of the organization.

OVERSEEING THE PERFORMANCE OF THE BOARD

Making Sure Board Meetings Are Efficient

The task of running meetings is usually left to the chair of the board. However, if attendance is dwindling and board members observe that meetings are boring, confusing, or contentious, and the chair's best efforts to make changes are not working, the governance committee may be able to help.

If it is apparent that meetings are not going well, but it is uncertain what the exact problem is, just ask. Instead of putting people on the spot, the governance committee can provide a meeting evaluation that each board member can fill out privately and anonymously after the meeting and return it to a member of the governance committee afterwards. The committee, in conjunction with the board chair, can work together to figure out what is going wrong and how to correct it. (Please see Appendix II for a sample meeting evaluation sheet.) In line with its responsibility of preventing problems on the board, the committee might suggest using meeting evaluations on a regular or periodic basis just to keep the board on its toes.

Keeping the Board Active and Engaged

The governance committee can be a resource for help not only in making sure board members understand what their roles and responsibilities are, but ensuring that each member is equipped with the tools she needs to ask questions, engage in stimulating discussions, and spread the word about the organization.

CASE STUDY: DID WE ELECT THE WRONG MEMBERS?

The Healthy People Project receives a hefty grant from the state health department. In return, the health department wants to nominate two members to the Healthy People Project's board. The board accepts the department's nominations, but it is soon apparent that the two new members are not active, rarely come to meetings, and, in general, are not particularly invested in their new appointments.

What's wrong with this picture?

Often public money comes with a request for the funding agency to nominate one or more board members. This control mechanism allows the funder to follow more closely how the organization handles the finances. While funders may provide expertise and, of course, access to needed income, they may also change the dynamic of board discussions or the culture of the board. Before accepting the funds, the board must be aware of the consequences on board composition.

In this situation, where the board must receive funder-nominated board members, the governance committee should guide them through the same process as other board members of explaining board expectations, orienting them, and ensuring that they are comfortable with the culture and work of the board. If they turn out to become uninterested in the board work and assigned duties, the board chair or chief executive should approach the funder and suggest that other individuals who are more likely to participate be nominated.

What now?

Ask the uninvolved board members, in a nonthreatening way, why they have not been participating. Ask if there are any board activities that they might be particularly interested in. Find out what they get excited about and involve them in that. Offer to provide a special orientation for them, personal tours of the organization's facilities, or a chance to meet some of its clients. Remind the uninvolved board members of their legal duties and suggest that it might not be wise for them to stay on the board if they are unable to exercise their duty of care. If, after all that attention, they still do not care to participate actively, go to the agency and suggest that it elects new representatives and allows your governance committee to be an integral part of the appointment process.

The governance committee can suggest innovations in board communications to the board chair and chief executive. Ask board members how much information they want and in what format. Many boards now have gone paperless and send out agendas and all board materials in e-mail. If your organization wants to try this, make sure every member has access to the appropriate technology. Some boards give their board members e-mail addresses, as well as access to and training on computers to make sure they can receive the information. It is important if you are doing board business electronically to establish policies governing e-mail discussions and votes so that everyone understands what is and is not allowed.

It could also be helpful to include a board development moment at every board meeting. This can be just a few minutes in which the board learns about some aspect of governance. Different members of the board should be recruited each time to lead the board development moment. This educational tool could cover an aspect of board bylaws that is unfamiliar, information about a promising practice that another board engages in, or a chance for the board to brainstorm about a new way of working. Implementing a small piece that strays from "business as usual" can make a big difference in board meeting dynamics.

Assisting the Full Board in Removing Noncontributing Board Members

The worst-case scenario: Suppose, despite all efforts, you end up with a board member who just does not fit in. You thought when you recruited him that he would be a perfect fit — but he is not. He is (choose one) too loud, too bossy, too lazy, too argumentative, too irresponsible, too absent — you name it. His presence at board meetings hinders progress and his presence on the board is starting to drive other board members away. Do not stand for a situation such as this one. The worst you could do is wait around until this individual ruins your board. If the board and organization are not happy, chances are the individual is not happy either and the best thing for everyone is to part ways amicably. The governance committee cannot remove board members, but should work closely with the board chair in exploring problems, options, and possible solutions.

Before a situation as unfortunate as this one ever has a chance to occur on your board, it would help to build a clause into your bylaws about how to remove a board member who is not working well with the rest of the board. This will provide preparation for when a worst-case scenario does arise. Periodically, provide board members with a way to evaluate their own participation in the work of the board, so you do not have to. Board members who do not feel fully engaged but would like to be more involved may jump at the chance to articulate what they are looking for in board participation or to be given the option of gracefully resigning their seat without feeling guilty.

As hard as it may seem, the board chair, with the support of the full board, can ask the troublesome board member to step down. It should come to this only after, of course, he has been offered every conceivable diplomatic option. When nothing else works, be honest but tactful; thank him for his service but state firmly that the board no longer requires his service. Dismiss this board member in as kind and respectful way as possible in order to avoid burning any bridges — but definitely do it, because you do not want to burn your board either.

TRY THIS!

Make sure that a governance committee member communicates with every leaving board member — whether he or she leaves because the term is up, for personal reasons, or has been asked to resign. Exit interviews can be quite revelatory as the pressure to manage relationships no longer exists. At that point it is generally easier to reflect on the past years and comment on future ideas for the board. Discuss quality of board orientation, suggestions for helping new board members, ideas for improving present board processes, and the member's major disappointments during the stay on your board. Get positive feedback on personal satisfaction and constructive criticism to help the governance committee focus on future improvements.

Preparing For and Conducting a Board Self-Assessment

Every few years, the governance committee should encourage the board to conduct a self-assessment. This can be accomplished, usually using an outside consultant, with the help of a variety of tools designed specifically for this purpose. A self-assessment is an effective way for the board to evaluate its effectiveness and help find ways to improve, whether it has developed dysfunctional patterns or whether it is simply striving for excellence.

Whatever self-assessment method or instrument your board chooses, it should be administered confidentially by a neutral third party so board members will be more likely to express their true feelings about both the good and bad parts of the board. Board members should be given enough time to complete the evaluation and should understand exactly what it is going to be used for and that their feedback will in no way be used against them.

When the results of all board member comments are tabulated, a skilled facilitator should be enlisted to analyze the data and present it to the board, usually at a board retreat or in a setting other than a regular board meeting. This way the board can devote its full attention to the self-assessment and what opportunities or challenges its results present to the board. It is important that board members focus on the future of the organization and the board's role in leading it rather than on themselves or interpersonal board issues. A self-assessment can help synthesize board members' opinions and feelings about the style or work of the board so they can step back and gain a clearer perspective on the board as a whole.

Benefits of a Board Retreat

One great way to strengthen the board is by holding an annual board retreat. Held at a site away from the usual boardroom, a retreat can provide the board with a thoughtful way to look at organizational strategy in a relaxed and comfortable setting. It is possible for a board or staff member to lead a board retreat, but, under most circumstances, it is preferable to recruit outside help. A neutral facilitator can help the board explore whatever issues are at hand without a personal agenda. The governance committee should work with this facilitator to create an agenda for the retreat that combines strategic issues with an opportunity for board members to socialize and get to know each other better.

If board members are willing to spend an entire day offsite at a retreat, make sure part of that time is spent having fun — either at lunch or with a team-building exercise or game in which everyone can participate. Starting the day off with an icebreaker will help set the tone for a productive but enjoyable work day. Be sure to provide plenty of healthy snacks as well, to fortify good thinking. Some boards find it particularly useful to go away for an overnight retreat because of the added opportunities for relaxed socializing and team building.

The governance committee can use a retreat as a way to gather information about the board's interests and the gaps in its members' knowledge. A retreat can help the board set direction for the future, or learn more about its current state. A retreat can be a good setting to discuss the results of a board self-assessment or to brainstorm about how to improve board effectiveness. A variety of results can come from a good retreat, and no particular agenda is better than another. Just make sure the retreat will address the issues most germane to the board at this particular time.

MANAGING OBEDIENCE TO THE ORGANIZATION'S MISSION

Providing Members with a Board Handbook and Action Calendar

A board handbook is the kind of tool that serves board members from the first week of their service to when they have expended their time and contribution to the board. Every board member needs a compilation of documents that serves as a quick reference on what he needs to know and remember about the organization, his own role, other board members, policies and processes for board function, and structural elements that define the board. More specifically, the handbook contains committee and task force job descriptions, board statement of responsibilities (including individual member responsibilities), articles of incorporation and bylaws, the strategic plan, the IRS Form 990 and the latest audit, any investment policies and other policies pertaining to the board (insurance, legal liability, etc.), a current funder list, a sample grant proposal, etc.

Creating an action calendar can help the governance committee stay on track and ensure that the board pays attention to necessary legal, financial, and other tasks in a timely manner. This calendar is an effective way of reminding board members of what they either have to implement themselves or ensure that they get implemented by staff before deadlines. The necessary elements to incorporate into the action calendar include:

1. Filing requirements

- File your Form 990 and 990-T on time by the 15th day of the fifth month after the fiscal year is over.

- If you raise funds in another state, file your annual reports — or register — in appropriate states.

- Withhold and pay employee taxes according to the IRS schedule.

- If you receive government funding, file your necessary reports.

2. Annual operational activities

- Evaluate the performance of the chief executive.

- Conduct an independent audit.

- Have board members review and sign their conflict-of-interest disclosure forms.

- Towards the end of the year, approve the budget for the coming fiscal year.

- Organize an annual board retreat.

- Review contracts and other agreements for their applicability.

- Assess the validity of your present investment policy.

3. Other possible activities

- Review your bylaws.

- Conduct board self-assessment.

- Review applicability of your strategic plan.

Assessing the Bylaws

It is quite possible that your organization's bylaws have not been revised for a long time — or ever. Bylaws should be a living document that accurately reflects the authority, processes, and the structure of the board. Every few years the bylaws should be examined to make sure they are easy to understand, relevant, and include the most up-to-date legal requirements of nonprofits. Ensuring that this happens could be a task assigned to the governance committee, but the implementation belongs to a special task force designated by the board.

Besides keeping an eye on bylaws clauses that seem outdated, create confusion, or are missing altogether, the governance committee's key role regarding bylaws is ensuring that all board members are aware of the contents of the organization's bylaws and understand how their actions are governed by them.

IRS Form 990

The governance committee may take it as a task to ensure that every board member is familiar with the Form 990 and to schedule a time in a board meeting for the full board to review it. Whether the form is prepared by a staff member, an outside accountant or another financial consultant, or by the board's treasurer, the entire board should see the form before it is submitted to the IRS, with each board member understanding what it says. What the 990 says about the organization can make a big difference to members of the media or the public who read it. There are ways to use the 990 as a positive public relations tool, so the board should make sure that opportunity is maximized.

Conflicts of Interest

Every board must struggle with conflicts of interest one time or another. There is nothing improper about a conflict of interest — it is a natural occurrence on all boards — unless it is not managed correctly. The governance committee can educate the board about the need for a solid policy and separate disclosure statement. They both provide a framework for the board to monitor its members' independence and impartiality when making decisions.

A conflict-of-interest disclosure statement is the place where board members reveal their relationships with people and other organizations that may compete with the interests of their organization. However, just because a board member has a possible conflict of interest does not mean she cannot ethically or legally serve on the board. It simply means she should be open about such relationships in case a potential conflict should arise.

How Does the Governance Committee Promote Ethical Behavior?

While the governance committee cannot and should not be accountable for the actions of the full board or its members, the committee's role is to ensure that the board has its own operational policies and procedures in place and that everyone understands them. These policies should reflect the values and ethical standards that the board has adopted.

Anytime an individual representing a particular organization, company, or government agency misbehaves or engages in wrongdoing, it reflects badly on that organization. Particularly in the nonprofit sector, which is so often misunderstood by the public and the press, we must redouble our efforts to demonstrate the good faith, good work, and good behavior of nonprofit board and staff members. Promoting ethical behavior on the board is an important job for the governance committee. One way to do this is by developing a code of ethics that everyone in the organization, including board, staff, and volunteers, must adhere to. It is important for the governance committee to use peer-to-peer self-regulation in this task — it is unfair to ask the chief executive to take this on. Please see the following figure for a sample code of ethics.

> **CODE OF ETHICS FOR BOARD MEMBERS**
>
> - Selflessness — Make decisions in terms of public interest, not private benefit.
>
> - Integrity — Serve the organization, not a third party.
>
> - Objectivity — Make unbiased decisions based on accurate information.
>
> - Accountability — Earn the public trust by standing behind your actions.
>
> - Openness — Share information willingly and clearly.
>
> - Honesty — Declare conflicts of interest. Do not hide the bad news.
>
> - Leadership — Promote, support, and follow organizational values.

It also may be helpful for the governance committee to promote adoption of certain standards of conduct in the boardroom, in addition to your code of ethics. In keeping civility in the boardroom, acceptable behavior standards are not tied to any parliamentary order. They are common-sense, often unwritten rules that allow your board meetings to proceed with courtesy and good humor. The following list provides some helpful tips:

- Arrive on time; stay until the end.
- Prepare for the meeting by reading materials.
- Don't use judgmental statements.
- Talk about issues, not people. Don't interrupt.
- Don't criticize those who are absent.
- Don't monopolize conversation.
- Avoid side conversations.
- Ask questions when you do not understand. There are no stupid questions.
- Keep confidential information confidential.
- Raise concerns in the boardroom, not in the parking lot afterwards.
- Recognize when you have a conflict of interest and disclose it to the group.

In keeping with the standards of conducts and/or a code of ethics, board members, and specifically committee members, help to ensure the stability, viability, and accountability of the organization they are governing. As "obvious" as these necessary actions may be, it is helpful to keep written documents that remind all members of the importance of demonstrating commitment and civility, both in the boardroom and in relationships with one another.

Conclusion

Maybe your board has managed just fine all these years without a governance committee. Why should you start one now? Because even if things work well on your board, they might work even better, and easier, with the help of a committee that supports and sustains the important work of the board. The governance committee can help the board plan for the future, which many boards do not have the luxury of doing when they are focused on keeping up with day-to-day operations. The governance committee can help the board stay organized and keep board members feeling energized and engaged in the organization's work.

Starting a brand-new committee with such a comprehensive mandate may seem daunting, but it won't be if you take it one step and one task at a time. The governance committee is organic to the board and will soon seem like it has always existed.

Depending on what stage of development your board and organization are in, a variety of missions and goals may be appropriate for your governance committee. Each board must decide for itself what charge it will give the governance committee this year, whether that will change the following year, and so on. The board should look to the governance committee as a resource, and the governance committee should change and evolve as necessary to help the board move forward.

The governance committee can be particularly useful in helping the board to succeed in the following:

- Plan ahead for recruiting new members.
- Recruit a balanced and inclusive board.

- Update its policies and bylaws.
- Ensure that new board members are oriented and engaged.
- Evaluate and improve its own performance.
- Promote ethical behavior among its members.
- Be accountable.

While the full board is ultimately responsible for its own actions and its own success, the governance committee can be an excellent mechanism to prompt the board to act and to suggest ideas and innovations.

A strong board can propel an organization forward to help it better serve the community, the nation, or the world. Creating and maintaining such a board is no small challenge in an environment of continuous change and scarce resources. An effective governance committee helps the board to rise to the challenge.

Appendix I

CHARGE TO THE GOVERNANCE COMMITTEE[1]

The Governance Committee is responsible for ongoing review and recommendations to enhance the quality and future viability of the board. It focuses on the following five areas, with specific duties dependent on board needs at any specific time, as well as evolving practice:

1. **Board Role and Responsibilities**

   - Lead the board in regularly reviewing and updating the board's statement of its role and areas of responsibility, and the expectations of individual trustees.

   - Assist the board in periodically updating and clarifying primary areas of focus for the board — the board's agenda for the next 1–2 years based on the strategic plan.

2. **Board Composition**

   - Lead in assessment of the current and anticipated needs for board composition. Determine the knowledge, attributes, skills, abilities, influence, and access the board will need to consider the issues that will arise in the foreseeable future.

   - Develop a profile of the board as it should evolve over time.

   - Identify potential board candidates, present them as possibilities, and explore their interest and availability (i.e., establish a pool of candidates).

   - Nominate qualified individuals under criteria to be elected as board trustees.

   - In cooperation with the board chair, contact each board member to assess his/her continuing interest in board membership and the term of service. Work with each director to identify the appropriate post (director role) she/he might assume.

3. **Board Knowledge**

   - Design and oversee a process of orientation, including information prior to election and during first cycle of board activity for new members (usually one year).

---

1. Adapted from *Transforming Board Structure: Strategies for Committees and Task Forces.* Washington, DC: BoardSource, 2001.

- Design and implement an ongoing program of board information and education.

4. Board Effectiveness

- Initiate the periodic assessment of the board's performance. Propose, as appropriate, changes in board structure, roles, and responsibilities.

- Provide ongoing counsel to the board chair and other board leaders on steps she/he might take to enhance board effectiveness.

- Regularly review the board's practices regarding member participation, conflict of interest, confidentiality, etc., and suggest improvements as needed.

- Periodically review and update the board's policy guidelines and practices.

5. Board Leadership

- Take the lead in succession planning, e.g., recruit and prepare for future board leadership.

- Nominate board members for election as board officers.

Appendix II

SAMPLE BOARD MEETING EVALUATION [2]

	OK	Needs Improvement	Suggestions for Improvement
1. The agenda was clear, supported by the necessary documents.			
2. The agenda was circulated prior to the meeting.			
3. All board members were prepared to discuss materials sent in advance.			
4. Reports were clear and contained necessary information.			
5. We avoided getting into administrative/management details.			
6. A diversity of opinions was expressed and issues were dealt with in a respectful manner.			
7. The chair guided the meeting effectively.			
8. Board members participated responsibly.			
9. Next steps were identified and responsibility assigned.			
10. Most board members were present.			
11. The meeting began and ended on time.			
12. The meeting room was conducive to work.			
13. We enjoyed being together.			

---

2. Hughes, Sandra R., Berit M. Lakey and Marla J. Bobowick. *The Board Building Cycle.* Washington, DC: BoardSource, 2000.

Suggested Resources

Andringa, Robert C. and Ted Engstrom. *Nonprofit Board Answer Book: Practical Guidelines for Board Members and Chief Executives.* Washington, DC: BoardSource, 2001. BoardSource has created the next best thing to sitting down face to face with thousands of board members and chief executives! Our new revised edition of the best-selling *Nonprofit Board Answer Book* is organized in an easy-to-follow question and answer format and covers almost every situation you're likely to encounter in nonprofit board governance, from structuring a board for success to nurturing strategic alliances with other organizations. Also included are action steps, real-life examples, and worksheets.

Axelrod, Nancy R. *Advisory Councils.* Washington, DC: BoardSource, 2004. This book expands the traditional way of looking at the concept of advisory councils, exploring ways in which they can help the board to keep its own magnitude in check without losing impact. Nancy Axelrod proves that these groups have more functions than usually assigned, and explains the role an advisory council can play in helping your board to expand outreach efforts, find new supporters, incorporate new perspectives, and distribute tasks.

Bobowick, Marla J., Sandra R. Hughes and Berit M. Lakey. *Transforming Board Structure: Strategies for Committees and Task Forces.* Washington, DC: BoardSource, 2001. This book provides a fresh look at committees and how your board can use work groups to streamline the work of the full board. Discover the importance of reducing the number of standing committees and relying more on ad hoc groups and task forces.

Fletcher, Kathleen. *The Policy Sampler: A Resource for Nonprofit Boards.* Washington, DC: BoardSource, 2000. In addition to steering the nonprofit organization's activities, nonprofit boards are also responsible for setting policies that govern their own actions. This resource provides nonprofit leaders with more than 70 sample board policies and job descriptions collected from a wide variety of nonprofits. The user's guide provides a basic overview for each of the policies. The diskette contains the full selection of sample policies and job descriptions that can be easily customized to suit your organization.

Hughes, Sandra R., Berit M. Lakey and Marla J. Bobowick. *The Board Building Cycle: Nine Steps to Finding, Recruiting, and Engaging Nonprofit Board Members.* Washington, DC: BoardSource, 2000. This book provides helpful tips on what motivates people to join boards, how and where to find board members, ideas for conducting an orientation session, and specific tasks for the board's governance committee. Also included are suggestions for involving former board members as advisors of committee members and removing difficult or ineffective board members. Included with *The Board Building Cycle* is a CD-ROM containing worksheets and forms.

Ingram, Richard T. *Ten Basic Responsibilities of Nonprofit Boards.* Washington, DC: BoardSource, 2004. More than 150,000 board members have already discovered this #1 BoardSource bestseller. This newly revised edition explores the 10 core areas of board responsibility. Share with board members the basic responsibilities, including determining mission and purpose, ensuring effective planning, and participating in fundraising. You'll find that this is an ideal reference for drafting job descriptions, assessing board performance, and orienting board members on their responsibilities.

Light, Mark. *Executive Committee.* Washington, DC: BoardSource, 2004. Executive committees are known to take on too much power, often resulting in confusion among the rest of the board members. Find out in which situations executive committees may be beneficial, and in what circumstances they may be a hindrance. Also included in this book is a description of who should serve on this committee and the intent of the committee's relationship with the board.

McLaughlin, Thomas A. *Financial Committees.* Washington, DC: BoardSource, 2004. Accountability is increasingly important to nonprofits, and every board must be engaged in understanding its fiduciary duties. Learn about the core responsibilities finance, audit, and investment committees can hold. Faced with the important task of fiscal oversight and safeguarding an organization's assets, it is imperative that finance committee members comprehend the scope of their responsibilities. Discover how these committees can address challenges in helping the rest of the board understand complicated fiscal issues. This book will also help finance committees to stress the importance of board member independence in oversight and audit functions, and prepare the board to address potential new legal regulations.

Presenting: Board Orientation. An Introductory Presentation for Nonprofit Board Members. Washington, DC: BoardSource, 2001. *Presenting: Board Orientation* is a ready-made, customizable, on-screen presentation that can be used as a traditional Microsoft® PowerPoint® graphics presentation, as overhead transparency slides, or printed out for handouts. Each slide is accompanied by a set of presentation notes and talking points to guide the discussion. Also included is a 16-page user's guide with suggestions for a board handbook, instructions for customizing the presentation for your board, and tips for a successful board orientation or recruitment session.

Tempel, Eugene R. *Development Committee.* Washington, DC: BoardSource, 2004. Motivating board members to be actively involved in fundraising is one of the greatest challenges nonprofit charities face; learn how a development committee can help with this challenge. This book clarifies the role of development committees, outlining how they can help with fundraising goals by serving as the board's internal fundraising trainer, motivator, and overseer, and including a discussion on the committee's relationship with development staff and an introduction to the use of organizational development committees.

About the Authors

Sandra R. Hughes is executive consultant for BoardSource. Sandy facilitates and leads programs on strategic thinking and planning, resource development, emerging trends and best practices, organizational culture and values, board restructuring, change, teamwork, effective meetings, and other topics.

Previously, Sandy held a variety of senior management positions with nonprofit organizations, foundations, and universities, including the United States Rowing Association, the American Bar Association, the Levi Strauss Foundation, and the University of Tennessee. Sandy holds a bachelor's degree in English from the University of Maryland. She also holds a master's degree in counseling and a doctorate in administration and organizational behavior from Northern Illinois University.

Berit M. Lakey is senior consultant for BoardSource. Berit provides individualized board consulting and training, conducts workshops for board members and board consultants, and is responsible for the BoardSource board self-assessment program.

Berit's career has connected her with health and human services organizations as well as with foundations and associations, both on the local and the national level. She has served as teacher, senior administrative staff member, executive director, and board member. In addition to her work with BoardSource, she has served as an adjunct assistant professor in the graduate school at the University of Maryland University College. The author of several publications on governance, Berit holds a bachelor's degree in sociology from Midland Lutheran College, and a master's degree in organizational development and a doctorate in human and organizational systems from the Fielding Institute in Santa Barbara, California.

Outi Flynn is director of knowledge dissemination at BoardSource and has been part of staff since 1989. For the past several years she has developed, structured, and managed the Board Information Center, one of the most highly utilized and popular services BoardSource offers.

Outi has created and contributed to the bulk of the governance information available on BoardSource's Web site, including topic papers and frequently asked questions, and acts as the primary content reviewer for the organization's publications. Her areas of expertise cover overall sector issues, dilemmas that concern nonprofit leaders on a daily basis, and structural and procedural challenges that affect board productivity. Outi holds a bachelor's degree in nutrition from Framingham State College.